GODS & GODD...
OF THE ANCIENT WORLD

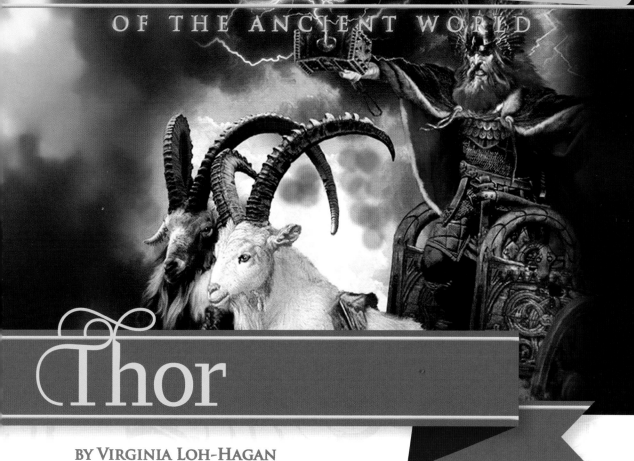

Thor

BY VIRGINIA LOH-HAGAN

Gods and goddesses were the main characters of myths. Myths are traditional stories from ancient cultures. Storytellers answered questions about the world by creating exciting explanations. People thought myths were true. Myths explained the unexplainable. They helped people make sense of human behavior and nature. Today, we use science to explain the world. But people still love myths. Myths may not be literally true. But they have meaning. They tell us something about our history and culture.

45th Parallel Press

Published in the United States of America by Cherry Lake Publishing
Ann Arbor, Michigan
www.cherrylakepublishing.com

Content Adviser: Alexandra Krasowski, Worcester Art Museum, Harvard University (Extension School)
Reading Adviser: Marla Conn MS, Ed., Literacy specialist, Read-Ability, Inc.
Book Design: Jen Wahi

Photo Credits: © Soerfm/Wikimedia Commons, 5; © Vuk Kostic/Wikimedia Commons, 6, 29; © Jopics/
Shutterstock.com, 8; © Vadym Farion/Shutterstock.com, 11; © Yevhenii Chulovskyi/Shutterstock.com, 13;
© Barandash Karandashich/Shutterstock.com, 15, 25; © Elmer Boyd Smith/Public Domain/Wikimedia Commons, 17;
© Esteban De Armas/Shutterstock.com, 19; © Fotokostic/Shutterstock.com, 22; © Howard David Johnson, 2018,
Cover, 1, 21, 27; Various art elements throughout, Shutterstock.com

45th Parallel Press is an imprint of Cherry Lake Publishing.

Library of Congress Cataloging-in-Publication Data

Names: Loh-Hagan, Virginia, author.
Title: Thor / by Virginia Loh-Hagan.
Description: Ann Arbor : Cherry Lake Publishing, 2018. | Series: Gods and goddesses of the ancient world |
    Includes bibliographical references and index.
Identifiers: LCCN 2018003334 | ISBN 9781534129443 (hardcover) | ISBN 9781534131149 (pdf) |
    ISBN 9781534132641 (pbk.) | ISBN 9781534134348 (hosted ebook)
Subjects: LCSH: Thor (Norse deity)—Juvenile literature.
Classification: LCC BL870.T5 L64 2018 | DDC 293/.2113—dc23
LC record available at https://lccn.loc.gov/2018003334

Printed in the United States of America
Corporate Graphics

ABOUT THE AUTHOR:

Dr. Virginia Loh-Hagan is an author, university professor, former classroom teacher, and curriculum designer. She thinks Chris Hemsworth was the perfect actor to play Thor. She lives in San Diego with her very tall husband and very naughty dogs. To learn more about her, visit www.virginialoh.com.

TABLE OF CONTENTS

CHAPTER 1

A FAMILY OF GIANTS

Who is Thor? Who are his family members? What was his connection to giants?

Thor was probably the most famous **Norse** god. Norse means coming from the area of Norway. Norse people were **Vikings**. Vikings traveled by sea. They raided. They attacked. They were warriors. They believed in many gods. They loved Thor best. Thor protected them. He helped them fight in wars.

Thor was the god of thunder. He was the god of lightning.
He was the god of storms. He was the god of strength.
He was the god of **fertility**. Fertility means the ability to
make babies. It also means the ability to grow crops.

Thor was a sky god.

Gods and giants hated each other.

Thor's father was Odin. Odin was the father of all gods. He was the father of all humans. He was called "All father." He married Frigg. Frigg was the goddess of marriage.

Odin wanted a special son. He wanted a powerful son. He wanted a son whose power came from the earth and sky. Odin went to the land of giants. He fell in love with

Jord. Jord was the goddess of earth. Jord gave birth to Thor. Odin took Thor to his home. Frigg acted like Thor's mother. Years later, Thor learned about Jord.

Family Tree

Grandparents: Borr (god of mountains), Bestla (giantess, goddess of water and ice), Nott (goddess of night), and Anarr (name means "another")

Parents: Odin (father of gods) and Jord (giantess, goddess of earth)

Half brothers: Baldur (god of light, peace, and summer sun), Hod (god of winter and darkness, often called Hodr), Hermod (messenger of the gods), and Heimdall (guardian of the gods)

Spouse: Sif (goddess of earth, wheat, fertility, and family)

Children: Modi (god of battle), Magni (god of strength), Thrud, and Ullr (stepson; god of archery)

A **giantess** is a female giant. Odin's mother was a giantess. Thor's mother was a giantess. This means Thor came from a family of giants.

Thor married Sif. They were a good match. Sif was a goddess of fertility, too. She had long, golden hair. Her hair looked like a field of wheat. Thor brought rain. He helped wheat grow.

Sif had a son named Ullr. Thor loved his stepson. Thor and Sif also had a daughter. Her name was Thrud.

Thor fell in love with Jarnsaxa. Jarnsaxa was a giantess. They had a son. The son was named Magni. Thor fell in love with another woman. They had a son named Modi.

 Ullr was the god of archery. Archery is the art of using bows and arrows.

CHAPTER 2

WORLD'S BODYGUARD

What does Thor look like? Where does Thor live? What are his good deeds?

Thor was huge. He ate a lot. He had red hair. He had a red beard. He had fierce, red eyes. Some stories say he had lightning in his eyes. He was stronger than any human. He was the strongest god. He could lift heavy things. He could kill big animals with his bare hands. He crushed mountains.

He was powerful. He was a good fighter. He was loyal. He was honorable. He kept communities safe. He kept out evil forces. He protected mankind. He protected **Asgard**.

Asgard was the universe's center. It was heaven. It was where the Aesir gods lived. There were two tribes of Norse gods. They were the Aesir and the Vanir. Giants wanted to attack Asgard. Thor's job was to keep them out.

Thor and his family lived in the biggest house. It was named Bilskirnir. This means "lightning crack." It was called the "place of might." It had 540 rooms. Thor kept his family safe.

Thor lived in Thrudheim.

All in the Family

Jord was Thor's mother. She was a giantess. Her father was Nott. Nott means night. Her mother was Anarr. Anarr means another. There aren't many stories about Jord. She was important for giving birth to Thor. She was Odin's lover. Odin was a sky god. Jord was goddess of the earth. Their union was powerful. Together, they created world balance. They made the land rich. They brought sun. They brought rain. They brought life. Thor loved his mother. He loved earth more than any other god. He loved the beauty of earth. He loved the power of earth. He protected the earth. He protected his mother.

The gods' grand houses were called halls.

Thor helped people. He guided sailors home. He made gentle winds. He started and stopped storms. He got rid of frost and ice. He brought warm spring rains.

Thor also has the job of **hallowing**. Hallow means to honor. It means to give blessings. Thor hallowed places. He hallowed things. He hallowed events, like weddings. This gave good luck to the bride and groom. He also hallowed lands. This made the land fertile.

CHAPTER 3

THE OTHER SIDE OF THOR

What are some of Thor's flaws? What are his weaknesses?

Thor wasn't the smartest god. He was not dumb. He was just not that wise. Many gods liked to trick him. They teased him. They made him into a fool. This made Thor mad. He had a bad temper. He was quick to anger. He raged. He ranted. He was always ready to fight. He didn't know how to take a joke.

Thor also didn't understand poems. Words confused him. Thor was in a contest. He fought against Odin using words. Odin was in a disguise. He pretended to be a boat worker. Thor lost.

Loki was a trickster god. He and Thor were in many stories together. Loki tricked Thor. He lied to him. He cheated him. But Thor fought back. He was the only god who could fight Loki. He was also able to capture him.

Odin was a wise god.

Real World Connection

Allen Pan is an inventor. He is an engineer. He calls himself an "imagination man." He said, "I try to make pretend things into real things!" He made a light saber. He made Captain America's shield. He also made Thor's hammer. He made a drone to control the hammer. He made a special backpack. The backpack has hand controls. This is how the hammer moves. Pan pilots the hammer back to his hand. He also made the hammer heavy. He said only one who was worthy can lift it. The hammer has special magnets. It sticks to metal surfaces. It can only be released by the right thumbprints on its handle. The hammer would only release with Pan's thumbprint. He played a trick on people. He put it on a busy street. He recorded people trying to lift it. Then he lifted it himself. He showed off. He thought it was funny.

Loki liked playing tricks.

Thor could be tricked with magic. He was fighting a giant. He couldn't kill him. The giant had magic. He could push away Thor's punches. Thor didn't know what to do.

Thor was always ready for an adventure. He liked showing off. Sometimes, he would go too far. He attacked without thinking. He focused on destroying his enemies.

CHAPTER 4

THUNDERING THOR

What are Thor's weapons? Why are his goats special?
Who are his servants?

Thor's hammer may be more famous than Thor. Thor's hammer was named Mjollnir. It was a magical hammer. It was the most powerful weapon. It was deadly. It was built by **dwarfs**. Dwarfs were magical creatures. They were known for mining. They were known for making magical weapons.

Thor would throw his hammer. It would cause lightning flashes. His hammer crushed things. This made the sound of thunder. Thor threw it into battle. It killed giants. It killed anything in its way.

Thor wore a magical belt. The belt doubled his power. Thor also wore magical iron gloves. The gloves helped

Thor used his hammer to hallow things.

Thor handle the hammer. The hammer had a short handle. Thor never went anywhere without his weapons.

Chariots are carts with two wheels. They're pulled by animals. Thor rode through the sky in his chariot. The noise from the wheels made thunder. The sparks from the wheels made lightning.

Goats pull his chariot. His goats were named Tanngrisnir and Tanngnjostr. Tanngrisnir means "teeth **snarler**." Snarl means to show teeth. Tanngnjostr means "teeth **grinder**." Grind means to rub things down.

Thor's goats were magical. They could be killed. This could happen over and over again. Thor used his hammer. He touched their bones. He touched their skin. This made the goats come back to life.

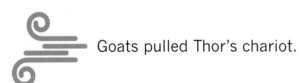
Goats pulled Thor's chariot.

Thor would sometimes seek revenge.

Thor and Loki spent the night at a farm. Thor killed his goats. He shared the meat. He shared it with Thialfi and Roskva. They were the children of farmers. They were **siblings**. Siblings are brothers and sisters.

Thialfi took one of the leg bones. He sucked out the **marrow**. Marrow is the stuff inside of bones. Thor brought the goats back to life. One goat had a broken leg. Thor got mad. He blamed Thialfi. He punished him and his sister. Thialfi and Roskva became his servants. They did whatever Thor wanted.

Cross-Cultural Connection

Indra was a Hindu sky god. Most Hindu worshipers are from India. Indra was the king of gods. He was the king of heaven. He was the god of lightning. He was the god of thunder. He was the god of rains. He was the god of river flows. His weapon was the thunderbolt. His throne was on storm clouds. His clouds were like divine cattle. Thunder was the sound of Indra fighting demons. Demons were always trying to steal the clouds. Rain was the sound of Indra milking his clouds. He was kind. He was helpful. He brought peace. He helped soldiers in war. Like Thor, his enemy was a snake. Vritra was a demon. He had 99 coils. He blocked up rivers. He caused a drought. Droughts are dry seasons. Indra killed Vritra with his thunderbolt.

CHAPTER 5

THOR'S WORST ENEMY

Who is Jormungand? What are some stories about Thor?

Midgard was earth. It's where humans lived. Jormungand was Thor's enemy. His name means "huge monster." He was a big sea snake. His body wrapped around Midgard. He was in the oceans. He held his tail in his mouth. He swallowed giants. He had sharp teeth. Poison dripped from his teeth. Jormungand's father was Loki. His mother was a giantess.

There are several stories about Thor and Jormungand. There was one story about fishing. Thor went fishing with a giant. The giant was named Hymir. They were in a boat. Thor used an ox's head as bait. He hooked Jormungand.

He pulled up the fishing pole. He had a hard time. His feet pushed through the boat. He braced his feet on the bottom

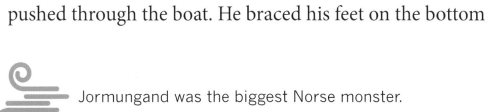
Jormungand was the biggest Norse monster.

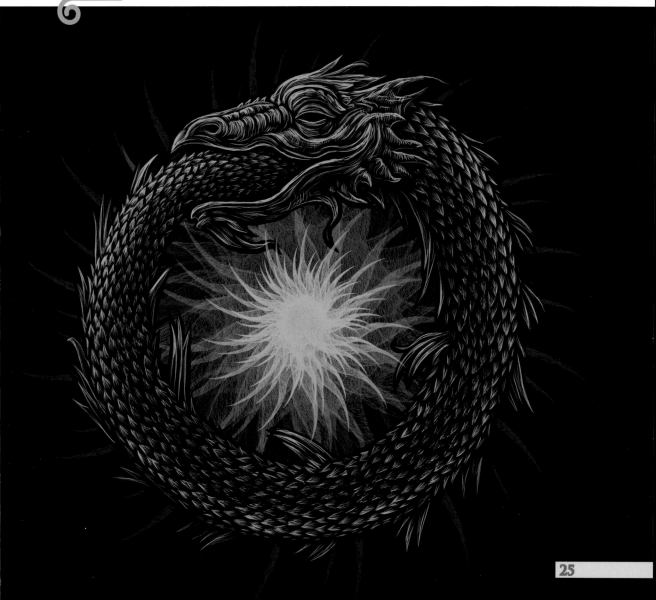

of the sea. He kept pulling the fishing line. Jormungand fought back. They tugged back and forth. Thor lifted his hammer. He was about to kill Jormungand. Hymir saw the monster's teeth. He got scared. He cut the fishing line. Thor threw his hammer. But Jormungand got away. Thor blamed Hymir. He threw Hymir into the sea.

Another story was about Thor's death. Thor fought in **Ragnarok**. It was the end of the world. It's known as the "doom of the gods." It happened after Baldur was killed. He was the god of light. His death caused 3 years of winter. It caused Ragnarok.

Jormungand got bored. He lived through 3 years of winter. He released his tail. He headed to the surface.

 Jormungand was also called the world serpent.

His movements caused earthquakes. They caused flooding. Jormungand planned on poisoning the sky.

Explained By Science

Thunder is a sound. It's caused by lightning. Lightning is a bolt of electricity. It shoots through the air. It makes the air vibrate. The vibrations are heard as sound. Lightning is very hot. The heat increases pressure. It increases temperature. Heat pushes air out. Air expands quickly. The surrounding cooler air gets heated up. This heat moves very quickly. It pushes apart the air. It uses great force. This movement makes a shock wave. It's like an explosion. Each shock wave takes a different amount of time to reach ears. The first shock wave can be heard 30 feet (9 meters) away. At the most, thunder can be heard 12 miles (19 kilometers) away. It can be a short, loud crack. It can be a long, low rumble.

Ragnarok was also known as the final battle.

Thor fought Jormungand. He used his hammer. He crushed Jormungand. But he walked back nine steps. He fell to the ground. He choked on Jormungand's poison. He died.

Don't anger the gods. Thor had great powers. And he knew how to use them.

DID YOU KNOW?

- Thursday was named after Thor.

- Many Vikings named their children after Thor. They also wore necklaces with Thor's hammers.

- Thor has at least 14 names. There are many stories written about him.

- Odin had many lovers. He had many sons. This means Thor had many brothers. But he was the most famous of Odin's sons. He helped Odin rule the world.

- Thrud may have been a Valkyrie. Valkyries are angels of death. They fly over battlefields. They take dead souls. They give half to Odin. They give the other half to Freya.

- After Thor died, his sons inherited his hammer.

- A dwarf wanted to marry Thor's daughter. Thor tricked him. He asked the dwarf many questions. He kept him up all night. Then the sun rose. The dwarf turned into stone.

- There were some temples in Sweden. These temples worshiped Thor. Huge hammers were kept there. People beat the hammers against drums. This made the sound of thunder.

- The giant Thrym stole Thor's hammer. He wanted to marry Freya. Thor dressed up as a bride. He dressed up as Freya. Thor tricked Thrym. Thrym used the hammer to hallow the wedding. Thor grabbed the hammer. He smashed the giant's head.

- A dwarf was making Thor's hammer. Loki dressed up like a bug. He bit the dwarf's eyelid. The dwarf messed up. That's why Thor's hammer has a short handle.

CONSIDER THIS!

TAKE A POSITION! Thor was Odin's most famous son. He was an important figure in the Norse myths. Research more about Odin's children. Do you think Thor deserves the attention he gets? Why or why not? Argue your point with reasons and evidence.

SAY WHAT? Reread chapter 5. Who was Thor's enemy? Compare Thor and his enemy. Explain how they're the same. Explain how they're different.

THINK ABOUT IT! Thor was known for his hammer. Why was his hammer so important? How does his hammer help him? If you could have your own special weapon, what would it be? Be creative.

LEARN MORE

Crossley-Holland, Kevin, and Jeffrey Alan Love (illust.). *Norse Myths: Tales of Odin, Thor and Loki.* Somerville, MA: Candlewick Studio, 2017.

Lunge-Larsen, Lise, and Jim Madsen (illust.). *The Adventures of Thor the Thunder God.* Boston: Houghton Mifflin, 2007.

Napoli, Donna Jo, and Christina Balit (illust.). *Treasury of Norse Mythology: Stories of Intrigue, Trickery, Love, and Revenge.* Washington, DC: National Geographic, 2015.

GLOSSARY

Asgard (AHS-gahrd) center of the universe where the Aesir gods lived

chariots (CHAR-ee-uhts) two-wheeled carts pulled by animals

dwarfs (DWORFZ) magical creatures who mine and make magical weapons

fertility (fer-TIL-ih-tee) the ability to make babies or to grow crops

giantess (JYE-uhn-tis) female giant

grinder (GRINDE-ur) a person or thing that rubs things down

hallowing (HAL-oh-ing) the act of blessing

marrow (MAR-oh) the substance inside bones

Norse (NORS) coming from the Norway area

Ragnarok (RAHG-nuh-rok) the final battle of the gods' world, marking the end of their world

siblings (SIB-lingz) brothers and sisters

snarler (SNAHR-lur) a person or thing that shows teeth

Vikings (VYE-kingz) seafaring warriors who raided and attacked towns

INDEX